Amazing AUSTRALIAN Women

TWELVE WOMEN WHO SHAPED HISTORY

Dedicated to my sisters – two amazing Australian women. PF

Dedicated to the littlest girl who is reading this by torchlight and dreaming of big things (yes, you!). Keep on dreaming. SB

A Lothian Children's Book

Published in Australia and New Zealand in 2018
by Hachette Australia
Level 17, 207 Kent Street, Sydney NSW 2000
www.hachettechildrens.com.au

10 9 8 7 6 5 4 3 2 1

Text copyright © Pamela Freeman 2018
Illustrations copyright © Sophie Beer 2018

This book is copyright. Apart from any fair dealing for the purposes of private study, research, criticism or review permitted under the *Copyright Act 1968*, no part may be stored or reproduced by any process without prior written permission. Enquiries should be made to the publisher.

 A catalogue record for this book is available from the National Library of Australia

ISBN 978 0 7344 1845 6 (hardback)
ISBN 978 0 7344 1847 0 (paperback)

Thanks to Vicki-Laine *maikutena* Green, the traditional custodian of Tarenore's story.
Designed by Christabella Designs
Colour reproduction by Splitting Image
Printed in China by Toppan Leefung Printing Limited

Introduction

In this book you'll meet twelve amazing Australian women who have changed the world, in small ways and large.

Some of them are famous around the world, such as Annette Kellerman and Nellie Melba.

Some of them are famous in Australia, such as Mary Reibey and Edith Cowan.

And all of them *deserve* to be famous, and admired.

They represent the warriors, artists, business owners, scientists, singers, politicians, actors, athletes, adventurers, activists and innovators of Australia. There are many more stories like theirs in our history. Perhaps one day *your* story will be one of them.

NOTE: People of Aboriginal and Torres Strait Islander heritage are advised that this book contains names and images of people who are deceased or may be deceased.

MARY REIBEY
CONVICT & BUSINESSWOMAN (1777–1855)

Mary Haydock was a daring and clever English girl. When she was thirteen, she dressed up in boys' clothes, called herself James Burrow and went for a ride on a horse a friend had lent to her, not knowing it was stolen. She was arrested for horse theft – they only found out she was a girl at her trial! Mary was transported to New South Wales as a convict, arriving in Sydney in 1792.

On the ship, she met Thomas Reibey, and two years afterwards they were married. Together they built a business importing goods by ship, as well as running several farms on the Hawkesbury River; Mary also ran a hotel.

When both her husband and his business partner died, Mary took over the business and built it into one of the most important organisations in the early colony. She was the first great businesswoman of Australia, which is why her portrait is on the $20 note!

TARENORE

(ALSO KNOWN AS WALYER)
INDIGENOUS RESISTANCE FIGHTER (C.1800–1831)

Tarenore was a Tomeginee woman from Emu Bay in Tasmania, born only three years before the first Europeans arrived on the island.

In her teens, Tarenore was abducted and sold as a slave to European seal hunters working in Bass Strait. Brave and resourceful, she learned English quickly and watched how the hunters used firearms.

Tarenore escaped, taking all the weapons and gunpowder she could find, and led a guerilla resistance movement against European invasion. She taught Indigenous fighters how to use muskets, and her band of warriors fought the British from the hills. She became their most dangerous enemy.

Although she was captured again and put to work to catch seals, her captors didn't realise who she was for some time. When they did, they separated her from other Aboriginal people to stop her from organising a revolt. Fierce and brave, Tarenore was a warrior through and through.

(Note: may also be spelled Tarenorerer, or Tarenorere.)

MARY LEE
SUFFRAGIST (1821–1909)

South Australia was a world leader in allowing women to vote, and the first place in the world where women could stand for election to Parliament. How did that happen?
Women like Mary Lee, that's how.

Mary Lee and other women (and some men) started the South Australian Women's Suffrage League in July 1888, to fight for women's rights. Mary was active, intelligent, outspoken and a great strategist – above all, she was totally committed to the cause.
'My aim is to leave the world better for women than I found it,' she said.

Mary was one of the founders of the first Working Women's Trade Union, and promoted better education for girls. But she knew the right to vote was the most important step in achieving equality. She spoke at hundreds of meetings, wrote articles and letters to newspapers, and lobbied governments and other opinion leaders.

Finally, in 1895, South Australian women over the voting age of twenty-one were granted the vote and the right to stand for Parliament.

Because women in South Australia and Western Australia already had the vote when Federation happened in 1901, all Australian women gained the right to vote in federal elections (state elections took a little longer).
So, women all over Australia owe a debt of thanks to Mary Lee and her colleagues!

NELLIE MELBA
OPERA SINGER (1861–1931)

'If you wish to understand me at all, you must understand that first and foremost I am an Australian,' Nellie Melba said. Maybe that was why she chose 'Melba' as her stage name in honour of her hometown, Melbourne. (Her real name was Helen Porter Mitchell.)

In 1904, Nellie Melba was called 'the world's greatest singer'. At one opera performance, seven kings and queens were in the audience – they had come from all over Europe to hear her sing.

She was fêted in Paris, London, Berlin and New York, but Nellie came home to Australia as often as she could, touring not just the big cities, but also country towns, large and small. She taught in Melbourne, without pay, to share her world-wide experience with younger Australian singers.

Ambitious, hard-working, generous (but occasionally ruthless to her rivals), Nellie Melba was one of the great stars of her time, renowned for the purity and beauty of her voice.

EDITH COWAN
POLITICIAN (1861–1932)

Edith Dircksey Cowan was the first woman in Australia to be elected to Parliament. She was voted in as a Member of Parliament (MP) in the Western Australian Parliament in 1921.

That on its own would have made her amazing, but her whole life was dedicated to the needs of women and children. From starting one of the first daycare centres for the children of working mothers, to becoming a magistrate, from promoting good free education to working for women's rights, Edith never stopped.

In fact, she really didn't stop – she became a Member of Parliament when she was almost sixty!

And after she lost the next election, she continued her life of public service in every possible way, fighting for women's rights and the welfare of children right up until her death in 1932.

One of her greatest achievements was the establishment of the Children's Court in 1907 – up until then, children had been treated as adults if they committed a crime, and were often sent to adult gaols. Edith Cowan's efforts made the lives of thousands of women and children better.

TILLY ASTON
TEACHER, WRITER AND DISABILITY ACTIVIST (1873–1947)

As a very young girl, Tilly Aston could see just a little — but by the time she was seven, she had mostly lost her sight.

She was determined not to let that stop her, and it didn't. The turning point was when Tilly learned Braille, which allowed her to study at the Victorian Asylum and School for the Blind.

Tilly became the first blind person in Australia to go to university, and the first blind teacher. Not only that, she began the organisation we know as Vision Australia *and* the first Braille library in the country.

Tilly was a central part of the movement to allow blind people to vote (gained in 1902 as part of Federation), to obtain free movement around the country, to receive free postage for Braille books, and to access a government pension.

As well as all this, she was a writer, who published six books of poetry and prose!

ROSE QUONG
ACTOR, LECTURER AND WRITER (1879–1972)

Rose Quong was born in Melbourne, and loved elocution and acting. She starred in a number of productions and loved acting in Shakespeare's plays.

When she went to London to expand her career, however, she found that the London theatre did not want a Chinese-Australian actor to play traditional 'European' roles. She decided, with encouragement from friends, to turn her ethnicity to her advantage, and became a lecturer on Chinese culture and literature, in theatres and on the radio.

Rose was so successful that she toured not only Britain, but also the United States – and even China. Her translations of Chinese works were widely used, and she helped encourage Western audiences to understand and appreciate Chinese literature, plays and music. She was intellectually brilliant and deemed 'an exceptionally fine lecturer' by reviewers, and audiences loved her.

Rose said, 'Strange as it may seem, many English and American people know almost nothing about China,' and she devoted most of her life to changing that.

ELIZABETH KENNY
NURSE AND MEDICAL INNOVATOR (1880–1952)

'It's better to be a lion for a day, than a sheep all your life.' That was Elizabeth Kenny's motto, and that was how she lived.

A bush nurse, she enlisted as an Army nurse in World War I and cared for wounded soldiers on hospital ships. After the war, she worked in rural Queensland at a time when poliomyelitis (polio) was beginning to spread. Polio is a disease that particularly attacks children and paralyses their muscles (which is why it was also known as infantile paralysis). There was a polio epidemic in the early twentieth century, which lasted until a vaccine was developed in the 1950s.

Elizabeth Kenny and a Queensland doctor developed a method of treating poliomyelitis patients that was the opposite of the official recommended treatment doctors used at the time. She set up clinics all over Australia. It took her years to convince the medical establishment that she was right – but she did, and in the process helped thousands of polio patients learn to move and walk again. She refused to give up until all polio patients were treated properly.

Sister Kenny, as she was always known, was invited to the United States, where she became famous for her innovative treatments and cures. Hollywood even made a movie about her!

ANNETTE KELLERMAN
SWIMMER AND MOVIE STAR (1887–1975)

Annette Kellerman came as close as anyone can to being a mermaid – she was called the 'Australian Mermaid' because of her success as a swimmer, movie actor and director, and performer all around the world. She invented the one-piece swimming costume for women, replacing the heavy woollen skirts and long-sleeved blouses women had worn to 'sea-bathe' – you couldn't swim properly in them! Wearing her new style of costume, she was arrested for indecency in America, but that court case established that the one-piece suit was acceptable in public, and women were set free to enjoy the water in the same way men did.

But when she was little, Annette couldn't even walk. At the age of two she had a disease called rickets, which meant she had to wear metal braces on her legs until she was seven. When the braces came off, a doctor advised her parents to have her swim regularly, and from that difficult start, she became a world-record-holding swimmer in the 100 yards and the mile!

Annette wrote and lectured about living a healthy life, encouraging women around the world to take up swimming and exercise, and made the Australian crawl (freestyle) a popular swimming stroke.

She performed in swimming and dancing exhibitions around the world, and starred in several movies – usually as a mermaid! Movie audiences loved her lithe and graceful swimming, and her clever choreography, which inspired the Olympic sport we know as synchronised swimming.

LORES BONNEY
AVIATION PIONEER (1897–1994)

Fearless, charming and determined, Lores Bonney was a pioneer pilot. In 1932, she flew all around the coast of Australia, setting a long-distance solo record that has never been beaten.

Then, she flew from Australia to England – the first woman to achieve this, despite mechanical trouble, a crash landing and damage to her plane. She almost flew into a mountain, but the clouds cleared just in time for her to go around it! She called her plane *My Little Ship*.

In 1937, in *My Little Ship II*, Lores became the first person to fly from Australia to South Africa, going up through Asia and down the east coast of Africa. No-one else has ever done this in a single-engine plane, to this day. She took a special frock with her to wear if she were invited to dinner along the way – and she was!

Lores's motto was: 'Don't let them tell you you can't do it!'

EMILY KAME KNGWARREYE
ARTIST (1910–1996)

Away out in the desert, seven hours' drive north of Alice Springs, around 1910, an Anmatyerre girl was born to Alhalkere country. She would come to be known as Emily Kame Kngwarreye, one of Australia's great artists.

Emily didn't start painting on canvas until she was in her seventies, at the Utopia community, which is a centre for art. Before that, she had led an adventurous life as a stockwoman on a pastoral property, and as a camel handler. She didn't let herself be tied into domestic service, which was the only work offered to poor country girls (especially Aboriginal girls) at the time.

Emily explained all her paintings of her country: 'Whole lot, that's the whole lot. Awelye (my Dreamings), alatyeye (pencil yam), arkerrthe (mountain devil lizard), ntange (grass seed), tingu (a Dreamtime pup), ankerre (emu), intekwe (a favourite food of emus, a small plant), atnwerle (green bean), and kame (yam seed). That's what I paint; the whole lot.'

Her work is now hung in galleries all around the world.

RUBY PAYNE-SCOTT
SCIENTIST (1912–1981)

Ruby Payne-Scott was the first woman to 'listen to the stars'.

After undertaking top-secret radar work during World War II, Ruby became one of the first radio astronomers in the world. At the CSIRO (the Commonwealth Scientific and Industrial Research Organisation), Ruby and her colleagues set up some of the earliest radio telescopes, and she led the work to define sunspots and their effect on the Earth. Among many other things, she discovered that the electromagnetic radiation given off by the sun's corona travelled through the solar system – and when it hit the Earth's magnetic field, it made the Northern and Southern Lights – the auroras. She and her team also discovered that the temperature of solar flares was over ten million degrees! Before that, people had thought the sun was only about six thousand degrees.

In Ruby's day, any woman who worked for the Public Service in Australia had to leave their job when they got married; so, Ruby kept her marriage secret for six years, until she was going to have a baby. She fought for equal pay for female scientists, and for equal work conditions, such as being allowed to wear the same type of clothes as the men. Confident, brilliant and supportive of social justice, environmental issues and women's rights, Ruby forged a path for other female scientists to follow.

There is a lot more to find out about every one of the women in this book – and many others. Here are some links to get you started.

MARY REIBEY

BIOGRAPHIES
adb.anu.edu.au/biography/reibey-mary-2583

www.bellsite.id.au/helen_tree/HTMLFiles/HTMLFiles_12/P5298.html

THE REIBEY INSTITUTE
www.reibeyinstitute.org.au/about/mary-reibey

MARY LEE

BIOGRAPHIES
adb.anu.edu.au/biography/lee-mary-7150

www.southaustralianhistory.com.au/lee.htm

IMAGES OF MARY
www.foundingdocs.gov.au/enlargement-eid-13-pid-10.html

EDITH COWAN

BIOGRAPHIES
www.womenaustralia.info/leaders/biogs/WLE0162b.htm

www.ecu.edu.au/about-ecu/welcome-to-ecu/edith-dircksey-cowan

IMAGES OF EDITH
www.nla.gov.au/nla.obj-136673287/view

TARENORE

BIOGRAPHIES
(Warning: adult content)
adb.anu.edu.au/biography/tarenorerer-13212

www.utas.edu.au/library/companion_to_tasmanian_history/W/Walyer.htm

www.fablecroft.com.au/books/cranky-ladies-of-history/cranky-ladies-of-history-guest-post-tarenorerer

NELLIE MELBA

BIOGRAPHY
www.womenaustralia.info/biogs/IMP0003b.htm

HER THEATRICAL HISTORY
www.liveperformance.com.au/halloffame/nelliemelba1.html

MELBA'S OBITUARY
www.oa.anu.edu.au/obituary/melba-dame-nellie-7551

TILLY ASTON

BIOGRAPHIES
www.womenaustralia.info/biogs/AWE2062b.htm

adb.anu.edu.au/biography/aston-matilda-ann-tilly-5078

IMAGES OF TILLY
www.victoriancollections.net.au/?q=tilly+aston

ROSE QUONG

BIOGRAPHY
adb.anu.edu.au/biography/quong-rose-maud-13162

AUDIO HISTORY
(emphasis on racism/bigotry)
www.abc.net.au/radionational/programs/pocketdocs/having-it-her-way-rose-maud-quong/7214654

ARTICLE
www.trove.nla.gov.au/newspaper/article/223604529?searchTerm=Rose%20Quong%20NOT%20

ELIZABETH KENNY

BIOGRAPHY
adb.anu.edu.au/biography/kenny-elizabeth-6934

IMAGES
Child patients at Sister Kenny clinic, Brisbane
www.archivessearch.qld.gov.au/Image/DigitalImageDetails.aspx?ImageId=3079

www.slv.vic.gov.au/pictoria/gid/slv-pic-aab62114

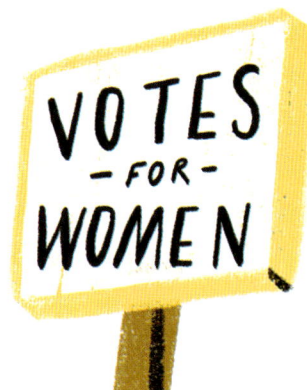

ANNETTE KELLERMAN

BIOGRAPHY
adb.anu.edu.au/biography/kellermann-annette-marie-sarah-6911

HER FILM CAREER
www.wfpp.cdrs.columbia.edu/pioneer/ccp-annette-kellerman/

WOMEN'S SWIMMING COSTUMES
www.clothe.net.au/terminology-tuesday-9-quirky-and-curious-fashion-terms-the-annette-kellerman-swimsuit/

LORES BONNEY

IMAGES
www.maas.museum/inside-the-collection/2012/03/08/celebrating-the-australian-aviatrix-lores-bonney/

HER FLYING LOG
www.nla.gov.au/nla.obj-235008454findingaid?digitised=y

ARTICLE
England trip www.trove.nla.gov.au/newspaper/article/192837071?searchTerm=Mrs%20Harry%20Bonney&searchLimits=l-category=Article||||l-decade=193||||l-year=1933

EMILY KAME KNGWARREYE

EMILY'S ART
www.artgallery.nsw.gov.au/collection/works/229.1992/

www.nga.gov.au/exhibitions/Kngwarreye

www.delmoregallery.com.au/pages/emily-kame-kngwarreye

IMAGES OF EMILY
www.trove.nla.gov.au/k/21898608?q=emily+kame+kngwarreye&c=picture&versionId=26376551

RUBY PAYNE-SCOTT

BIOGRAPHIES
www.womeninscienceaust.org/2016/09/20/the-life-and-times-of-ruby-payne-scott-1912-1981

adb.anu.edu.au/biography/payne-scott-ruby-violet-15036

www.naa.gov.au/collection/snapshots/find-of-the-month/2009-march.aspx

CONCLUSION

There are so many amazing Australian women, it was hard to select just twelve.

In every avenue of life, there are stories of women doing extraordinary things: brave, clever, generous, adventurous, kind, talented, hard-working, persevering people who changed their world.

So, ask yourself:

What is *my* story going to be?

What will *I* do?

How will *I* change my world?